NOW YOU CAN READ. . . .
WISE SOLOMON

STORY RETOLD BY LEONARD MATTHEWS

ILLUSTRATED BY MAURICE BROWNFOOT

Library of Congress Cataloging in Publication Data

Matthews, Leonard.
  Wise Solomon.

  (Now you can read—Bible stories)
  Summary: Retells the Old Testament story about
the deeds of the wise King Solomon.
  1. Solomon, King of Israel—Juvenile literature.
2. Palestine—Kings and rulers—Biography—Juvenile
literature.   3. Bible.   O.T.—Biography—Juvenile
literature.   [1. Bible stories—O.T.]   I. Title.
II. Series.
BS580.S6M37   1984   222'.530924   [B]   84-15903
ISBN 0-86625-310-6

Published by Rourke Publications, Inc., P.O. Box 3328, Vero
Beach, Florida 32964. Copyright © 1984 by Rourke Publica-
tions, Inc. All copyrights reserved. No part of this book may
be reproduced in any form without written permission from
the publisher. Printed in the United States of America.
  The Publishers acknowledge permission from Brimax
Books for the use of the name ''Now You Can Read'' and
''Large Type For First Readers'' which identify Brimax Now
You Can Read series.

GROLIER ENTERPRISES CORP.

NOW YOU CAN READ....

WISE SOLOMON

King David ruled over Israel for forty years. As a boy he had killed the giant Goliath and saved his people. When he grew up, he became king. His armies

fought many battles. David loved God. He wanted to thank Him for all the good things God had given him. He thought that he would build a great temple in praise of God. God loved David but He did not want His temple to be built by such a warlike man.

King David had a son. His name was Solomon. He became king after David died. Solomon was not like his father. He was not a soldier. He loved peace. While he was king, there were no wars in Israel. It was a time of peace and plenty.
This pleased God.

Solomon was a young man when he became king. His country had many enemies. Solomon thought, "How can I keep Israel from being attacked by its neighbors? I must find a strong friend. No one is more powerful than Pharoah, the king of Egypt." Solomon became the good friend of Pharoah. After a while he married the daughter of Pharoah. He brought his new wife back home to Jerusalem. What a welcome they were given!

The people of Israel greeted the happy couple with cheers and happiness. They knew now that Israel had a powerful friend. No enemy would dare to attack Israel. King Solomon was already proving he was a wise man. Still, the king had doubts about himself. He would often wonder, "Can I really rule over such a large country as Israel with so many people?"

Then came the time when King Solomon was in a city called Gibeon, which lay five miles to the north of Jerusalem. That night, while he was asleep, he had a dream. In his dream God came to him and said, "Solomon, I have been watching you. You have been a good king to your people. I am pleased with you. I wish to reward you for all the

good work you have done. Tell me what would make you happy?" To this Solomon replied, "A great king must know how to rule. I ask only for wisdom."

God was pleased that Solomon had not asked for riches and long life. "You will have a wise and understanding heart," God said. "Because you were not selfish, I will give you everything you have not asked for."

Then God said, "You will have riches, power and long life. You will be called 'Solomon the Wise'."

The next morning, when King Solomon awoke, his heart was filled with gladness. He knew that everything that God had promised him would com true. Solomon was right to have faith in God. As time went by he became a great and good king. All the world talked about him and how wise he was. Israel became a rich country.

All the people of Israel loved their king. They trusted him. They were sure that he was always fair and understanding.

Time went on and King Solomon grew in wisdom. He was always reading. He knew about trees and animals. He learned about birds and fishes. He knew everything that went on in his kingdom.

Wise and great men from other lands came to Israel to learn from King Solomon. Other kings visited him. They wanted to see how he ruled his kingdom. They saw how good life was for the people who lived in Israel and how happy they all were. The other kings wanted the same things for their own people. They listened to King Solomon.

"How wise he is," they all said. "He is the wisest of us all."

Then Solomon remembered the great temple that his father had wanted to build. Now it was time for him to thank God for his blessings. He made up his mind to build the temple.

Solomon called the finest builders to come and speak with him. He told them that he planned to build the greatest temple ever seen.

The builders nodded. Then one said "We must have cedar wood to build your temple but no cedar trees grow in Israel."

Solomon wrote a letter to Hiram, the king of Tyre. There were plenty of cedar trees growing in Hiram's country. Hiram had been a friend of David.

"You know," Solomon wrote, "that my father, David, had planned to build a great temple in praise of God."

Then Solomon wrote, " I am about to build the temple. My builders tell me we must have cedar wood but no cedar trees grow in Israel. In your country there are forests of cedar trees."

Solomon then offered to trade wheat, barley, wine and oil if Hiram would give him some of his cedar trees in exchange. King Hiram gave orders for many cedar trees to be chopped down.

"I am happy to help the great King Solomon," Hiram wrote back. "I am sending you many ships loaded with all the cedar wood you need to build the great temple."

Work soon started on the temple and crowds of people came from all over Israel to help with the building. They wanted to please their king.

Large stones had to be carried many miles to the site.

Only the finest wood and gold leaf were used. The temple was covered with gold inside and out. Great golden statues of angels stood on the roof.

It took seven long years before the
great temple was finished. Only the
best was good enough for God.
Inside the temple the Ark was placed.
The Ark was a box in which were two
stones. The Ten Commandments that
God had given to Moses were written
on those stones. The Ark was sacred
to the people of Israel.

The great temple of Jerusalem was the wonder of all Israel. When it was ready, King Solomon the Wise offered it to God.

"The God of our Fathers be with us," Solomon cried, raising his hands. "We pray He will never leave us."

All these appear in the pages of the story. Can you find them?

Solomon

Pharoah's daughter

David

King
Hiram

builder

woodcutter

bed

Now tell the story in your own words.